Neil Spirtas'

FLORIDA'S FORGOTTEN CRACKERS

Wider Perspectives Publishing, Norfolk, Va. 2021

FLORIDA'S FORGOTTEN CRACKERS

Poems by
Neil H. Spirtas

Except where noted as quotes, writings herein are the product of Neil H. Spirtas, and he is responsible for the contents. Wider Perspectives Publishing reserves 1st run rights of this work and all rights revert to the author upon delivery. Author then reserves the right to grant or restrict reprinting of this volume in whole or in part and may resubmit for contests and anthologies at will. Reproduction of the contents of this volume, in whole or in part, is only permissible with consent of the author.

Image *A Cracker Cowboy* by Frederic Remington care of *State Archives of Florida*

Neil Spirtas' own photography p. 7 & 32.

Skyshadow Photography's Emilio "Sonny" Vergara Photographs on covers & pp. 4 9 11 17 23 27 29 & 40

Paintings on pp. 20 & 35 by Herbie Rose

Art p. 25 by Gene Barber, in the Florida Department of State publication *Florida in the 1980s, Reliving the Past With Centennials*

Published by Wider Perspectives Publishing, Hampton Roads, Virginia
©Copyright Neil H. Spirtas January 2021
ISBN: 978-1-952773-31-0

Acknowledgments

The "*Mystical, Musical, Medicinal Manatee*" was previously published in a different adaptation entitled "*The Manatee River*" from my debut chapbook, **When Men Cry; Life's Later Voyages,** published by Wider Perspectives Publishing (WPP). A special thank you to James Wilson, Publisher of WPP.

My heartfelt gratitude to the following people for their encouragement, assistance, and ideas in the development of these poems and this chapbook.

To my mentors: C. David Anderson, M.B. McLatchey, Clara Macri, Ben Hyland, Sonny Vergara, Graciela Giles, Herbie Rose – of blessed memory, Peter Carlson, Lori Reiss, and Gene Barber – of blessed memory and truly the first Florida Cracker I have ever known.

To Emilio "Sonny" Vergara, owner of Skyshadow Photography, whose photographic and technical skills were tremendous in helping me to fill these pages with beauty and inspiration. The front and back covers display his abundant talent. His photos inside this book are black and white renderings of his art, observe his gift in living color at skyshadowphotography.com.

To Cracker aficionados, writers, and historians, Dana St. Claire, Patrick D. Smith – of blessed memory, Gilbert Smith, Dr. James Michael Denham, Libby and Joe Warner – of blessed memory, and Rick Tonyan. Truly inspirational people whom all blazed the Cracker trail and "on their shoulders" came before me.

To my wife, whose technical computer and social media skills are beyond comparison. Whenever I needed moral support, a second and valued opinion - she was there for me. This chapbook would not have been possible without her by my side. Her bringing me an occasional tea also kept me caffeinated for the task at hand.

Contents

Introduction	1
The Old Florida Cracker's Survived	3
What Went Down That Crooked River	6
Crackers in the Mist	8
Don't Be Fooled by Pierre	10
Saving the Osceola	12
Movin' On	14
The Mystical, Musical, Medicinal Manatee	16
Owning the Road	19
Tick-Tock	21
Triggers	22
Going thru Airport Security	24
Man Should Work	26
Six Inches Too Long	28
My First Cobia: Three Inches Too Short	30
Mullet Thieves	31
Snooty the Manatee	34
The Last of the Elephants	37
A Tale of Two Fishermen's Boats	38
Author's Concluding Note	40
About the Author	41
Testimonials	42

INTRODUCTION

This book is dedicated to and in celebration of a threatened way of life in Florida – a lifestyle still hanging on by the coattails of those Crackers and natives that inhabited its mostly rural areas. I have lived in the northernmost part of Florida, bordering the Florida-Georgia line; in southwest Manatee County, where the western Florida Cracker Trail ends; and in Hernando County – a small, rural Southern confine due north of Tampa. I am not a strong believer in labels, but most of my life has been in Florida, and I am proud to be classified as a Floridian.

Identifying with the Florida Crackers, I am but an observer, bearing witness. Self-sufficient, self-reliant on the bare necessities of life, and at times maligned – all characteristics I share with the Cracker described in these pages. Since Canadian poet Adam Sol described poetry as "the perfect language" my goal was to impart a Cracker-like painting onto this complex canvas.

L'dor v'dor is a Hebrew phrase that means passing "from generation to generation" – to our youth – important customs and traditions. My hope is to engage the reader in the life of Florida's settlers – some of their phrases and knowledge on safeguarding what remains the best of Florida.

By acknowledgment and appreciation of Florida's beginnings – its beauty, its current natural and man-made environment – the present-day challenges remain vast. Sage advice from Charles Dickens in 1870 were "*Be natural my children. For the writer that is natural has fulfilled all the rules of art*" from a 2011 The Times news article.

Population increases of 900-plus new residents daily have stressed the Florida of old. Just think of adding a new city the size of Orlando every year! Where is that new "place" to be located? Hopefully, this book opens some doors – new and old – for the critters, the Crackers, and the newbies to this pioneering state on ways to appreciate and to enhance our natural resources and heritage – not to exploit them.

A CRACKER COWBOY.

"What cracker is this same that deafes our ears with this abundance of superfluous breath."
– William Shakespeare, 1594

The Old Florida Cracker's Survived

> Cracker defined – a self-reliant, independent, and tenacious settler of the Deep South, often of Celtic stock; who subsisted by farming or raising livestock and, as a general rule, valued personal independence, civil restraint-free life over material prosperity – Dana Ste. Claire *

Wrapped up in today's energy
of the blinding city lights
engrossed with technology and
of grocery stores at every corner.

Tucked away many miles
from any civilization
ever wonder how Old Florida Crackers survived
without AC or electricity?

Comfortably curled up by a fiery fireplace flame
nearly a century and one half ago
when firewood and candles were necessities,
when meat and fish were hunted
then stored for the wintery season ahead.

Hanging on to
their Cracker culture
their folklore
their way of life.

Where trailblazing pioneers and drovers once walked
where poaching strangers now bought
where cattle crossed a vast, vanishing plain
where Cracker cowboys rounded up Spanish Andalusians and
where on their small, smooth-riding marshtackies*
they bolstered The Old Florida Cracker Trail -
blazing it back into glory.

Where the fresh waters of Lake Okeechobee,
where the rivers of the St. John's, St. Mary's
and Withlacoochee - supplied the life source for Cracker's to survive.

* *"The Old Florida Cracker's Survived"*. Author Dana Ste. Claire's enlightening and vivid account, ***Cracker; The Cracker Culture in Florida History***, 1998, The Museum of Arts and Sciences, Daytona Beach, Florida is one of several versions describing the Florida Cracker. Other definitions will be highlighted to reveal a backstory in this book. *Marshtachies were

small horses known for their stamina, maneuverability, and easy ride. Spanish descendants brought these horses to the state that were most well-suited to Florida's wilderness.

"Crackers aren't only part of Florida history. To a great extent, they are Florida history." Cracker is chic ... it is now a compliment to be referred as one. – Rick Tonyan, Writer, Author of Cracker Westerns

What Went Down that Crooked River

Native American Indians named it
the Big and Small River.
With sudden swells in the rainy season and
low lying waters in the dry -
water officials call it Crooked River.

So gentle as the river frequently flows
so crooked she bends and bows
so, whenever I go down to that raging, river's edge
I recall both her paths of peace
and her dooms of destruction.

Flowing down the dew-laden Withlacoochee River were
floating docks, beds, boats, and once
as I awoke, frolicking from afar
an antique, uncanny, upright rocker
in the grey of the misty, morning twilight.

If only I would have gaffed that rocker
as it approached ever so closely
as I refocused my eyes clearly.
So eerily, it resembled grandma's treasured
Wimbledon white rocker

Where mother sewed and read and
rocked in her bedroom:
same shape, same coloring, and all
swaying back and forth down the Withlacoochee
where the ospreys' screech and call.

What I really want to say
no one totally knows -
where these storied objects go
where they have been before destined
for Yankeetown ... into the Gulf of Mexico.

The word Crackers was first used in Florida in 1767 referencing a "Crackertown" settlement on the St. John's River near Palatka – Dana St. Claire, Author, Historian

CRACKERS IN THE MIST

The dissipating, sinewy dew
filled the morning river's path.
Melting in the misty, thin air
as the skies danced
their shimmering sparkle below.

Storytelling of Old Florida tales were on my mind
now soaking up an aroused air for a New Florida
as the birds' chirped resonating sounds
in our cul-de-sac
of Couvey's Cove.

The gator basked in the sun
ready to mate and pounce on any prying prey.
The cooters dove deep below
after catching their breath.
The "scrub chicken"* took to their burrows.

In the distance you could hear the lash
of the cowherder's crack * of his whip.
If you only knew how,
you could hear the faint sounds of
Crackers in the mist.

* *"Crackers in the Mist"*. Scrub chickens were gopher tortoises. This Cracker definition is the most popular; *"Well, people didn't know what cracker meant and they thought it was just a slang word, you know for a person. But it was named after the whip, I think, the cracklin' whip, as the cow hunters come in. There weren't cowboys in those days, there were cow hunters, and they used those whips and we'd say, "Yep, here comes the Crackers." That's where the word Crackers comes from. I'm always callin' myself a Cracker."* – Jesse Otis Beall, DeBary, Florida Cracker, 1997 ... quote from Ste. Claire's Cracker Culture book above.

Don't be Fooled by Pierre

> *- Florida Crackers never really ate much alligator meat. It was popularized in the 1950's and early 1960's.**

Relics and critters claim the river's banks
But not so long ago, Florida gators were nearly extinct
they are a protected species now
along with goliath groupers and cypress trees.

Lazily they wander along the crooked river
around the bend of what we've dubbed "turtle town".
Even with eleven cooter surrounding gator Pierre
the Withlacoochee River seems as silky smooth
as a baby's skin. Yet,
don't be fooled.

Now she rages like a bull,
albeit still one of God's peaceful kayaking experiences
you can hear the echoes of passersby
they resemble the sounds of kids playing peacefully
in your neighbor's backyard. Remember,
don't be fooled.

My wife and her friend
innocently named Pierre by a slip of the tongue.
You see ... Gators number
one for every fifteen Floridians,
in the first 25 feet are as fast as a horse
with their swift predatory bursts of speed. Cautious,
don't be fooled.

Shocked when I told him about Pierre
the state's alligator wrestling champion roared,
"You, are in big trouble" and continuing in his Cracker vernacular -
"naming a gator is akin to feeding him as one's pet ...
yet, go get, some good tennis shoes!"
Gapingly he bellowed ...
don't be fooled.

* *"Don't be fooled by Pierre"*. Alligators are not to be treated as household pets. Gator hunting was a way of life that helped supplement significantly

to the income of Cracker fishermen like Jesse Otis Beall. Originally, it was too heavy to tote the meat of an alligator, so it was sold primarily for the hides. The quote is paraphrased from an interview of fisherman Beall regarding gators by author Dana Ste. Claire, pages, 91-94 in *Cracker; The Cracker Culture in Florida History*.

SAVING THE OSCEOLA

Ivory-billed woodpeckers
Florida's black bears
Florida's stalking slew of panthers
soaring scrub blue jays and unhatched eggs of eastern Bluebirds
basked in the nation's forest of Osceola.

The nearby watering hole of Ocean Pond
expecting by locals to be reserved for generations to come
indefinitely halted for years and years and years with
"Phosphate's" veiled threat to strip mine the forest.

Then all at once a town of Babel was standing there
where individual rights were wagered against the public benefit
where deep in the devil's dreaded path
where one of the environment's last dinosaurs
fought the need
to feed the hungry.

Politicos Chiles* and Fuqua to the rescue
heeding the clarion call aimed at dwindling
phosphate tailings from filling the air and
to further forsake its namesake –
Seminole warrior Osceola.

Stripping the lands by the Leviathan's many hands
as its head hovered and homed in on its prey

until the lawyers and legislators had their day
in the court of Cracker heritage justice.

Photo courtesy Ed Chiles.

* "*The He-Coon walks just before the light of day.*" – Lawton Chiles, Florida's 41st Governor (referenced from his final debate with opponent Jeb Bush in 1994 for the Governor's race).

Chiles was U.S. Senator when he led the fight to save the Osceola National Forest in the early 1980's.

Movin' On

> *"To leave, a part of you dies ..."*
> – French proverb*

From urban canals to rural rivers
to sea level at sixty feet above

from Sunday morning bicyclists
to canoeists outside my back-porch window, I was movin' on.

From traffic jams just around the corner
to road rage a thing of the past

from my poolside Adirondack armchair
replaced by a veranda river view

from a 40's brick house
to a cabin in the woods on stilts

from being overwrought with activities
to a changed way of life, I was movin' on.

From a beloved barber
who always knew exactly what I wanted

to a clueless lady who, unaware
botched my hair, I was still movin' on.

"Just a trim," I said when asked about what kind of haircut I wanted,
lost in her conversation I became bewildered, then

suddenly the haircut was finished
she spun me around in her chair, "well what do you think?"

Unexpectedly, heatedly I hollered,
"I hate it!"

I resembled Moe, from the Three Stooges
with his symbolic-sculpted salad bowl haircut.

But despite the "one-day stand" lady barber
I was still ... movin' on.

* *"Movin' On"*. Have you moved recently to a new home, a new city or a new country? It is one of the major stressors in a lifetime. A thought-provoking and metaphoric quote that comes to mind is from the novel, ***A Land Remembered***, by Patrick D. Smith, published by Pineapple Press, 1984, pg. 201, "*To cry at parting would not be the way of an Indian (woman).*"

The Mystical, Musical, Medicinal Manatee*

> From Joe Warner's The Singing River
> – "Sounds filled the air when a young
> brave and his lovely maiden had
> a courtship ..."*

Life's changed on The Great River.
Nothing so beautiful than to be
on the mystical, musical Manatee.
With porpoises airborne and snook galore,
a romantical love affair – based on local lore.

The Spaniards and Indians claim its mouth,
according to history.
But no one owns it,
clones it,
controls its fury.

A river that flows with the sea
and the inland waters,
now near Lake Manatee,
whose natural bounty
fulfills loftier quarters.

Not only fishing smacks and ranchos of commerce and trade
not only a medicinal spring on its south bank
not only a romancing, musical river with surround sound
where a battle was fought,
where half of the Calusa and Timucuan tribes
on each side of the river were killed.

The Indians called it
"The Great River of the Mystic Music"
where the music sprang up from all directions
where her waves would ebb and crest
where she giveth and taketh away
among the very worst and the absolute best.

Poems are written by fools like me:
Only Nature could have made the
mystical, musical, medicinal Manatee.

"Look into nature and you will understand everything better."
– Albert Einstein

* *"The Mystical, Musical, Medicinal Manatee"* is inspired originally by one of my mother's, of blessed memory, favorite poems *Trees*, by Sergeant Joyce Kilmer. It was revised from "The Manatee River" poem in my inaugural chapbook, *When Men Cry: Life's Later Voyages*, to include the legend of the Manatee River. The following introductory Legend was found in Joe Warner's, ***The Singing River***, 1st printing 1986 and expounds upon a love story and magic of the river: "*As he clasped her tightly to his breast, a sound filled the air. It seemed to come across the water. The brave thought they had been discovered, as the sound came from everywhere;*

over their heads, around and around their bodies, then beneath them in the water. It was the most beautiful and lovely music. The maiden knew her brave to be mystified, and to soothe his alarm, she explained about the mysterious music that seemed to come from the Great River on certain moons. He was spellbound and thought because of their great love, the river was presenting them with a good omen."

Owning the Road

> Conversation by Sol MacIvey, in Patrick D. Smith's,
> **A Land Remembered** – " *Before it was finished (TamiamiTrail) in '28 (1928), it took ten days to cross the Everglades to Miami, and we made the same trip this morning in three hours.*"*

To those with their excessive speeding,
darting to and fro,
beware of their mode.
For they lay claim
to owning the road.

To those molding public opinion,
the sophists, the wielding power politicos -
road raging relentlessly a many from their elevated SUV's.

To those impatient and pouncing,
thru their bumper-to-bumper, highway antics –
the teenagers and the young,
rushing with their social media near at hand.
Then to the insouciant seniors – because
 most noticeably, they go too slow.

To those begrudging their middle years,
worker bees with their energy efficient autos.
The safety-conscious, the hybrid-users, the bikers, the bicyclists -
because of issues about fear and safety,
Big Brother and punctuality.

To those not owning up
to the rules of the road and coming for thee:
no one person owns – except ever so slightly,
the taxpayer,
you and me.

Neil Spirtas

Florida's Forgotten Crackers

* ***"Owning the Road"***. The verse is borrowed from a favorite quotation/ poem of mine by the Lutheran Pastor in Germany, Martin Niemoller who was best remembered by: *"First they came for the Communists and I*

did not speak out – because I was not a Communist. Then they came for the Socialists and I did not speak out – because I was not a Socialist. Then they came for the trade unionists, and I did not speak out – because I was not a trade unionist. Then they came for the Jews and I did not speak out – because I was not a Jew. Then they came for me and there was no one left to speak out for me." Another meaning of this poem deals with the possession of the "road". Material possessions meant little to the self-sufficient settlers - the Crackers. Possessions cannot be taken with you ... we only really own what we are willing to share – paraphrasing a Biblical reference.

Tick-Tock ...

The alarm clock buzzes, sun light arouses, seeping through tree and windowpane. Work beckons us to creation, at noon there's a luncheon, Jerry Seinfeld's on at seven. The tide soon rolls
in and out, and in and out again, while
the streams ripple ever so slowly
sleep suddenly emerges
cloaked by the
moonlight's
darkness.
Convention
and industrialization,
tick-tock we peer, as the five
AM hour rushes in, trying to escape the fog
later co-worker's forgotten goodbyes to their fellow men.
Starting all over, inhale a nautical musical attempt at the lunar calendar to hear the cardinals chirping and the whippoorwills wooing, exhale the metronome's tick-tock play breath in and out, in and out again, while you are awakening to the distant Gulf of Mexico roar.

TRIGGERS

> *"During the 1890's Arcadia (Fl.) averaged 50 gunfights per day, that action was all part of a 30-year war between cattlemen and rustlers along the ironically named Peace River."** - Rick Tonyan

Idle chatter,
bellowing banter,
chuckles emerge
into full blown laughter.

Swallow-tail kites hover,
schools of fish scatter.
Dolphins look, at times, as if to play,
in truth - to corner their prey.

Summer showers,
clockwork May's flowers,
Transcontinental divides,
shatter land mass on all sides.

The crack of the whip frightens,
catchdogs herd cattle,
The bass devour many minnows
before gators consume them, too.

Pens meet paper,
books prelude movies to deliver.
Arguments atrophy,
casualties result from catastrophe.

Peace petrifies
into wars to mend.
Violence triggers,
no man's friend.

* *"Triggers"*. From Foreword by Rick Tonyan in *Cracker, The Cracker Culture in Florida History.* The many quarrels sited in Arcadia were when there was a lawlessness and a time of great strife between rustlers and cattlemen. Fencing laws were not passed in Florida until 1949. All too often, these disagreements were settled by violent means. How different is this approach in still trying to resolve answers today, among and between countries of differing beliefs, political structures, and leaderships?

GOING THRU AIRPORT SECURITY

Ever wonder
what random sprays and lotions
containing dangerous chemicals,
may be lurking in your luggage?

Why your wife has been randomly and often
chosen by the psycho-security judges
to be frisked frequently and snatched sneakily
for sealed plastic containers of strawberry apple sauce?

Or that posh amplifying hair mousse taken
to the airport's land of the lost and stolen?

Your olive oil from Italy, a gift for your secretary,
gets pilfered by some security guard's heist.

Yet, where does it all go?

Maybe to flow,
mysteriously into the Cracker's cast iron skillet
somewhere, somehow,
who will ever know?

By Gene Barber
Signature artwork from the 1981 Glen St. Mary, Fl. Centennial

MAN SHOULD WORK

> *"When you reap the harvest of your land, do not reap to the very edges of your field or gather the gleanings of your harvest."* Leviticus 19:9 *

Badgers build their dams
Macaws make their nests
Snakes steal their offspring's eggs
Swans soar south.

Crows caw to protect their nest
Gators grunt and growl territorially
Pileate woodpeckers' peck prophetically
Whippoorwills' warn to call out their mate on steamy summer nights.

Firewood fields abloom
Afore the wintery storms blow.
Animals stay alive mouth-to-mouth
With mere sustenance to show.

Gloriously men craft castles
Iron domes to erect
Proudly and artfully to withstand
Legislation to deflect.

Man should strive to exceed labor
Giving back
While working to his hearts' content
While ultimately finding their edge to humanly perfect.

* *"Man Should Work"*. The Leviticus citation means to reap/ leave after your work and labor is finished, at "the corners" of your field for those more needy of the harvested (corn or olives, etc.). This type of charity is a just way of allowing those to come and partake without being seen or heard (at the corners or edges of the fields). Salvaging their humility.

SIX INCHES TOO LONG

No ease
to catch a Red at seas.
For months and months, he sought their holes,
baited their favorite foods,
prayed to the fishing gods.

Then, suddenly his cast dipped
a bee line to China.
The rig's drag was set,
the handle immobilized,
the rod bent 360 degrees.

What could it be?
A sleek shark, a pumping catfish?
Peering through the water's surface, all worn and wobbly,
he could see – a larger-than-life head,
a black spot tail Red.

"Too big!" jeered the skipper, as the shiny silver fish
made its way on board.
She affirmed apologetically – the biggest Red that she had ever seen.
This fish, caught with only half a shrimp,
was *six inches too long*.

With those four words declared,
the Red was returned
to the comfort of her cherished channel pass.
His day as a fisherman had reached a peaceful pinnacle
having caught so many bottom-eating, mudder cats.

My First Cobia; Three Inches Too Short

Whew ... what a catch
my line zooming toward Big Pass,
thought I lost him until looming
30 feet off the starboard bow

a Cobia sighting, circling
back and forth to stern again!

Settling under the hull
this rogue returned to starboard
ever so slightly showing off his colors
of blended black, white, and grey.

My hardest skirmish ever
was a clashing Cobia,
swashbuckling it's head to and fro'
surfacing, then out of view.

Get the net, get the net
I heard echoing ...
no, he's not ready yet!

Give him some time
the captain yelled, keep it tight,
he'll fool you, slash your line!

Still determined to shake loose by my giving and taking,
finally, ... he wore out.

Carefully reclaiming the king Cobia
measuring on the ship's floor,
I heard the skipper declare "three inches too small"
uttering under her breath "donkey of the sea" –
at which time I gladly let the colossal Cobia free.

Mullet Thieves

> *"By 1770, there were 30 or more ships actively engaged in the fishing operations on the west coast of Florida. Their daily catches of seabass, mullet, drum, pompano, swordfish, and trout were brought into the ranchos (early Spanish fishermen's shacks) and cleaned, salted, and dried for the Cuban market."* *

Three summers ago
poachers with their expansive nets
traveled to Florida's west coast
with one thing in mind,
the female roe.

But they forgot the males,
Left behind their corpses to float.
No labor force any longer
to take them back by boat. *
Let their gills fill with water
let their tails sway
and the oxygen flow.

Get thee to market mullet thieves
wasteful, aren't we?
Let's dodge this genocide!
Where, oh where, are we,
to find
the Green constituency.

* ***"Mullet Thieves"*** in its subtitled quote from Libby and Joe Warner's ***The Singing River***, pg. 4, shares the lively and productive fishing enterprises of the 18th century. The Cuban market was the destination with salted and dried mullet roe - especially being considered a delicacy. Even today the roe is a much-wanted commodity, however not to the destruction of the male partner and counterpoint being left behind. According to Warner, "*fishing ranchos became unprofitable during the cholera outbreak in Cuba in 1834.*" In the following year, with the termination of the Second Seminole War, the era of Spanish fishermen ended and most returned to Cuba (from the Manatee River area).

Florida's Forgotten Crackers

SNOOTY THE MANATEE

The longest living Manatee
no more.
A day, after his 69th birthday,
caught in his home waters,
drowned,
by no malice of others,
nor fate of his own.

Animal activists clamoring
for Snooty justice -
hometown folk that knew him,
came to honor him,
to praise him,
to love him,
notwithstanding, the early mystery*
behind that unlatched door.

Rin -Tin -Tin, Silver, Phil the Gorilla,
all departed icons of yesterday.
Snooty, soon... was bound to join someday.

I will always remember baby "Snoots" smiling
on his pool's ledge - greeting his fans,
eating veggies and pounds of lettuce
out of their sight - right out of their hands.

Sure, as he was the oldest living and safely born into captivity,
quietly he departed,
searching silently into the night.

"When a man knows he's going to die, he goes off into the woods ... searching for the place of his birth." – A Seminole Legend, from **A Land Remembered**

* *"Snooty the Manatee"* was the oldest and first known manatee born into captivity. He was world renown, loved by young and old, and died on July 23, 2017 – two days after his 69th birthday. According to an autopsy and investigative accounts in Bradenton, Fl., he died due to drowning when a latched door was accidentally left open and he was allowed access to an unsafe area. He represented Florida's efforts to educate and to protect this once endangered species.

THE LAST OF THE ELEPHANTS*

The hovering circus crowds wave by
to the giants just beyond the Midway.
Without a vote or a say,
to sway the mammoth headlines
of this demoted mammal.

Outdone by the courts of special interest justice.
Ancient power and behemoth strength
analogous to the turbulent times
of their closely related,
the threatened manatee.

Retire these megaherbivores, to lands
with their favorite fruits
with farms in our subtropics
with abundant trees and tables
full of their beloved luscious chulta.

Legalese or corporate greed?
Unshackled say the animal freedom lovers
saved from the poacher's rifles.
Apparently … they will never forget.

* *"The Last of the Elephants"* – The last performance of the Ringling Brothers circus was in May 2017. The 146-year-old show according to Feld Entertainment – who acquired the circus in 1967 – had been unable to recover from a drop-off in ticket sales when a year before they stopped elephants in the circus (and due to anti-circus and anti-elephant regulations in cities and counties).

A Tale of Two Fishermen's Boats*

Eagerly waiting for our boat and crew,
one day I encountered a most pleasing Cracker fisherman.
Excitedly he arrived at the bait shop.
Running out of shrimp and braid lines shredding,
he was catching a flurry of frenetic fish
yet losing them as fast as he was reeling them in.

"Where did you catch all those Redfish?" I asked.
Proudly, generously, he blurted out the exact location.

Without hesitating, we followed him to his hot spot
where every one of our crew all landed Reds.
Upon leaving the site he kindly asked,
"Do you want the rest of my shrimp?"
Obligingly, we accepted his live shrimp.

Advancing one month later
we returned to this magical hole to find two fishermen
stationed in our long-awaited site.
While we anchored accidentally nearby,
due to an unpredictable tide,
they barked,
in no uncertain terms,
telling us to leave.
Growling back at them we moved the anchor,
Never ... ever intending to hover so close
to horn in on "their" territory.

Such a tale of two fishermen...
one convivial, the other greedy
one sharing, the other meagerly
one insecure and protective,
the other open-armed and collected.

It was not the worst of times
as our skipper, caught the catch of the day, a 20-inch Black Drum. It was a far, far better thing, for example, that my grandfather did when he assumed the jailtime of his cousin's.

It will be a far, far better thing that we do
when a group of fishermen
cozy up to us, someday,
near this extraordinary fishing hole.

* *"A Tale of Two Fishermen's Boats"* has a couple of poetic suggestions. Both surround a similar, dramatic presentation that American poet and humanist Walt Whitman called "embracing multitudes". The Paris Review article on "The Art of Distance," 4/6/20, elaborated on this subject, *"Poems are also good at holding seemingly contradictory ideas and feelings in the same breath: I am afraid and hopeful, lonely and open hearted, stuck but not without my inner freedom."* Credit English novelist Charles Dickens best known for his "A Tale of Two Cities," and *"It was the best of times, it was the worst of times, it was the age of wisdom, it was the age of foolishness, it was the epoch of belief, it was the epic of incredulity,"* etc..
Specifically, Dickens' phrases were utilized twice in my last stanza both in the *'worst of times'* and *'it was a far, far better thing'* in referring to my grandfather, who apparently went to jail for a relative's crime. Of course, for those of you who remember Dicken's tale, it was a much more extraordinary life and death setting.

AUTHOR'S CONCLUDING NOTE

Most of the work in this chapbook includes water or fish-related poems. Florida is uniquely surrounded by water and remains a fishing capital. Both subject matters are very precarious, having been mentioned in the Bible 722 times (water) and in 24 verses (fish). The tales, parables, and history are vivid and many including Jonas and the Whale, the parting of the Red Sea, and Jesus' three followers all being fishermen. Because Florida Crackers and the Indian population greatly relied on water and fishing for their livelihoods and survival and the author's affection for both, you will find them dominating these pages.

- Ode to the Fisherman -
Lo, the fisherman,
Mighty are his preparations;
He rises early and goes forth,
Full of great expectations;
He returneth late,
Smelling of strong drink
And the truth is not in him. – Anonymous

About the Author

Self-admittedly, Neil Spirtas is no authority on Cracker lore. His first few professional jobs were in the rural hinterlands of southeast Missouri's "Lead belt" area, the coal-mining communities of southwest Pennsylvania, and northeast Florida in a county where "moonshine" stills existed as recent as the late 70's. History, culture, and customs have always intrigued this author.

With his undergraduate and master's in Community Development from the University of Missouri, Spirtas retired as an executive with the Manatee Chamber of Commerce after 30 years. In that period, he observed great growth and a doubling of the population.

Spirtas' community and historical work included; foreword and editing, *Florida in the 1980's: Reliving the Past with Centennials*, editing *The Magicians of Main Street:* America and its Chambers of Commerce, 1768 - 1945 by Chris Mead, and author of the Manatee Chamber's Quasquicentennial history in 2014.

His poetry can be found in Roam, Poetica, Free Expressions, The Soul's Bright Home, The Eclectic Muse: A Poetry Journal, & the Current magazines, The Huffington Post and his debut chapbook, *When Men Cry; Life's Later Voyages* by Wider Perspectives Publishing. Also find him in the upcoming HRAC volume: Our Decameron Days.

Testimonials

"Perhaps the most distinctive trait of a Florida Cracker is a deep connection with the land, the water, and other natural bounties of Florida. Neil Spirtas has gifted us with fine examples of this connection through what some might consider an unusual medium for Florida Crackers – poetry. All Floridians who treasure our state's unique landscape and culture will enjoy this fine collection."

- James M. Denham, Professor of History at Florida Southern College (FSC) and Director of the Lawton M. Chiles Center for History at FSC

"In Neil Spirtas' delightful chapbook the Cracker's connection with the land and rivers of Florida is brought lovingly to life with poetry, humor, photos, and informative documentary comment. We could use more of their independence and care for our natural beauties today."

-Peter Meinke, Poet Laureate of Florida

"With Neil Spirtas driving the cracker train, the words of *Florida's Forgotten Crackers* come to life as a Florida adventure. Through rousing poetic stories of real-life experiences, Neil teaches, entertains, and reminds us all why Florida is a special place in the south."

-Judge Gilbert Smith, Historian, Author of <u>Lawyers & Legends of Manatee County</u>

"As more and more of rural and small-town Florida falls victim to development, a small band of writers are trying to preserve the state's history and culture in words. Neil Spirtas is one of those. His eloquent poetic talent depicts what it is like to be a Cracker."

- Rick Tonyan, Writer, Author of <u>Cracker Westerns</u>

Florida's Forgotten Crackers

colophon
Brought to you by Wider Perspectives Publishing, care of J.Scott Wilson, with the mission of advancing the poetry and creative community of Hampton Roads, Virginia and poets of the wide, wide world.

See our production of works from ...

Edith Blake
Tanya Cunningham-Jones
    (Scientific Eve)
Terra Leigh
Ray Simmons
Samantha Borders-Shoemaker
Bobby K.
    (The Poor Man's Poet)
J. Scott Wilson (TEECH!)
Charles Wilson
Gloria Darlene Mann
Neil Spirtas
Zach Crowe
Jorge Mendez & JT Williams
Sarah Eileen Williams
Stephanie Diana (Noftz)
the Hampton Roads
    Artistic Collective

Jason Brown (Drk Mtr)
Martina Champion
Tony Broadway
Ken Sutton
Crickyt J. Expression
Lisa M. Kendrick
Cassandra IsFree
Nich (Nicholis Williams)
Samantha Geovjian Clarke
Natalie Morison-Uzzle
Gus Woodward II
Patsy Bickerstaff
Catherine TL Hodges
Jack Cassada
Dezz
Chichi Iwuorie

... and others to come soon.

We promote and support the artists of the 757
from the seats, from the stands,
from the snapping fingers and clapping hands
from the pages, and the stages
and now we pass them forth
to the ages

> Check for the above artists on FaceBook, the Virginia Poetry Online channel on YouTube, and other social media.

Hampton Roads Artistic Collective is an extension of WPP which strives to simultaneously support worthy causes in Hampton Roads and the local creative artists.

www.ingramcontent.com/pod-product-compliance
Lightning Source LLC
Chambersburg PA
CBHW051712090426
42736CB00013B/2667